IMAGES
of America

NORTH
ATTLEBOROUGH

MASSACHUSETTS

Lieutenant Robert F. Toner died in the service of his country. Prior to the United States entering World War II, Mr. Toner joined the Royal Canadian Air Force (he is seen here in his RCAF uniform). As part of an American Air Force crew on a bombing mission over Italy in April of 1943, he and his plane, "Lady Be Good," failed to return. The wreckage of the plane and the bodies of its crew were found in the Libyan Desert in 1959. A diary kept by Lt. Toner was found amongst the debris. It told of their struggle to stay alive and their hope for rescue. The last entry was made eight days after they crashed. The diary formed the basis of a *Life* magazine story, a book, and a television movie.

COVER PHOTOGRAPH: Joe Martin (at far right, holding the bat) is pictured with the high school baseball team at the high school on the corner of Broad and High Streets in North Attleborough. He received his first years of schooling at the School Street School, and eventually went on to serve in the U.S. House of Representatives from 1925 to 1966. He was the Republican leader for many of those years and Speaker of the House under Presidents Harry S. Truman and Dwight D. Eisenhower. (Photograph taken from a glass-plate negative in the collection of the Attleboro Industrial Museum.)

IMAGES
of America

NORTH
ATTLEBOROUGH
MASSACHUSETTS

Bob Lanpher, Dorothea Donnelly, and George Cunningham

Hope you
recognize a few places
Good Collecting,
Bob Lanpher

ARCADIA

First published 1998
Copyright © Bob Lanpher, Dorothea Donnelly,
and George Cunningham, 1998

ISBN 0-7524-0885-2

Published by Arcadia Publishing,
an imprint of the Chalford Publishing Corporation,
One Washington Center, Dover, New Hampshire 03820.
Printed in Great Britain

Library of Congress Cataloging-in-Publication Data applied for

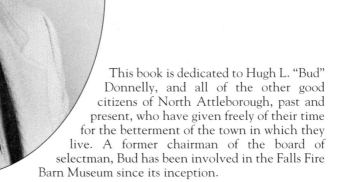

This book is dedicated to Hugh L. "Bud" Donnelly, and all of the other good citizens of North Attleborough, past and present, who have given freely of their time for the betterment of the town in which they live. A former chairman of the board of selectman, Bud has been involved in the Falls Fire Barn Museum since its inception.

Contents

Introduction

North Attleborough (part of the Rehoboth North Purchase of 1661) was originally part of the land incorporated as the town of Attleborough in 1694. In 1887 it was cleaved from that town and incorporated as a separate town. It was a close vote, but an overwhelming majority of those in East Attleborough, the section of town that would later become the city of Attleboro, voted that the two sections should be separated.

Within North Attleborough's bounds are the site of the original meetinghouse of the town of Attleborough and most of the oldest settled parts, including the section known as Oldtown and the site of Woodcock's Garrison at the North End. Despite these facts, East Attleborough retained the old town name of Attleborough and the incorporation date that went with it.

The earliest manufacture of jewelry in the United States was also within the bounds of North Attleborough. In 1780, "The Frenchman" manufactured jewelry on the property of Jesse F. Richards on South Washington Street, just south of the intersection of Chestnut Street. He passed his knowledge on to the residents of this town and they grew it into an industry. North Attleborough was also home to the earliest shop devoted to the manufacture of gilt buttons. John Daggett's *A Sketch of the History of Attleborough From its Settlement to the Division*, compiled in 1894 by his daughter, Amelia Daggett Sheffield, contains a detailed account of the early jewelry and button manufacturers.

North Attleborough has always been blessed with a fortuitous location, having been situated on the Old Bay Path from Massachusetts Bay to Narragansett Bay and later on the Norfolk and Bristol Turnpike and the Old Boston Post Road. The seeds of separation were sown with the establishment of the railroad through East Attleborough in the 1830s. Today, North

Attleborough is situated on Routes 95, 295, and 1, and is only a few miles south of Route 495.

The town has also been blessed with a good supply of water. The rivers once important to the early development of industry here now recharge the wells from which we draw our drinking water.

Perhaps most importantly, however, North Attleborough has always been blessed with a civic-minded citizenry and it is to them that we dedicate this work. The members of the North Attleborough Falls Fire Barn Preservation Society, Inc. hope that you enjoy this book and will take the opportunity to visit our museum.

The Falls Fire Barn served the residents of the town of North Attleborough for 84 years—from 1893 to 1977. After the building was abandoned as a fire station, it was used for storage until the firehouse was placed on the National Register of Historic Places and a committee was formed to "save the Falls Fire Barn." Through a variety of activities, money was raised to bring the building back to life. The museum now holds fire equipment, jewelry, Native American artifacts, photographs, books, letters, and most anything else that has a relationship to the history of our town and our region.

One
Going to School

This *c*. 1900 view looking southwest on May Street between Abbott Run and Adamsdale Road shows the Adamsdale School and the Frank E. Gay home. The schoolhouse replaced another that burned on this site in 1850. The North Attleborough Historical Society moved the schoolhouse to North Washington Street in the 1970s and added a cupola and bell to the structure. The original village name, Lanesville, derived from a Daniel Lane who owned a 52-acre farm here. In 1875 the name was changed to Adamsdale in honor of the Adams family of which John F. Adams, former mayor of Pawtucket and owner of the mill, was a member. (Photograph courtesy of the North Attleborough Historical Society.)

The first schoolhouse in what was then known as Lanesville was erected in 1805. The building was located on May Street between Abbott Run and Depot Street. It was later moved and used for storage for the Lanesville cotton mill.

Many children in this 1870s view of the Adamsdale School also attended Sunday school in the same building. The Cushman Union Sunday School started in 1860 and held regular services in the schoolhouse until the Cushman Union Chapel was completed in 1883.

When this photograph was taken in 1930, the Holmes School housed grades one through four. Each grade sat in a separate row of desks. The building, built in 1848, ended its days as a school in 1955. (Photograph courtesy of Robert Halliday Jr., third from the right in the front row.)

Attleborough gave the school districts the authority to raise money and build schools in 1804. District #1, now called Oldtown, was the first to do so in 1805. Oldtown encompasses the original settlement of the town of Attleborough, including the location of the first meetinghouse. The second Oldtown school building, built sometime after 1832, is currently owned by the First Congregational Church.

The New Boston School, originally located within the triangle of land bounded by Bungay Road and Kelley Boulevard, was moved to its present site on Bungy Road when Route 95 was constructed in 1960. John Daggett attended this school in the early 1800s. Classes continued here until 1926. The New Boston Community League acquired the building in 1927 and donated $10,000 from the sale of the school in 1987 to restoring the Falls Fire Barn.

The Mt. Hope Street School housed grades four through nine when it opened in 1893. The door on the left faced Mt. Hope Street; the right door faced Chestnut Street. Each floor contained two classrooms and a corridor that ran the length of the building. (An 1890s photograph, courtesy of the Attleboro Industrial Museum.)

The Towne Street School, built in 1849, was located on the northerly side of Towne Street just east of the intersection with Mt. Hope Street. In the 1930s and '40s the school housed grades one through three. (Photograph courtesy of Lillian Sumner.)

Miss Marian Gilmore started her long career of teaching in North Attleborough schools in 1929 with the second-grade class of the Towne Street School. From left to right are as follows: (front row) the Papineau twins—Harold and Henry, Rose Tollo, Esther Carlstrom, Doris Forbes, Norma Malinowski, Dorothy Bugbee, Dorothea David, Beatrice Melanson, and Rae Sprague; (middle row) George Babcock, Albert Anderson, Betty French, Alice Hagberg, Edward Zersky, Gertrude Arno, Lillian Weygand, Raymond Rogers, Harry Wilmarth, and Eugene Mobriant; (back row) John McGowan, Albert Desrosiers, George Lemire, Herbert Tyler, Stiles Simpson, Herman Nittel, and Thomas Wilmarth.

The Park Street School, built about 1850, was located on the westerly side of Park Street just north of the School Street intersection. The building was situated lengthwise on the lot, with the entrance facing School Street. This building replaced the original one-room school, now a residence, built in 1818. The school housed grades four through six in the 1920s.

Baseball was a popular sport when this picture was taken at the rear of the Park Street School about 1880. The fence, bisecting the lot, separated not only the boys' and girls' play-yards, but also their outhouses, which were a necessity in the days before indoor plumbing. Having closed for a short time, the school reopened to house junior high classes relocated due to a fire at the J.D. Pierce School on November 28, 1924. The Park Street School building was torn down in 1933.

Miss Nellie Capron's 1928 class at the School Street School included the following, from left to right: (front row) Glenys Howe, June Henshaw, Elton Duckworth, William Wing, Kingsley Enoch, Robert Benker, Edward Duckworth, Warren Hoffman, unknown, John Bouchard, and Charles Bates; (second row) Effie Hurkett, Ruth Waterson, Ellen Wilmore, Ruth Beaulieu, Evelyn May, unknown, Harriet Forbes, Louise Moore, Ann Gardiner, and Marilyn Smith; (third row) Doris May, Byron Schofield, Jeannette ?, Adele Miner, Marion Schickle, Alice Norman, Helen Collins, Helen ?, Evelyn Gagnon, Lois Swallow, Marjorie West, Rita Everton, Priscilla Rhind, and Barbara Ralston; (back row) Norman Sanford, Fred White, James Flood, Robert Everton, Kenneth Caswell, Donald Roessler, William Forbes, Frank Woodbury, Howard Hartman, Edwin Enoch, unknown, and Roger Benker. The School Street School, built in the 1870s, was located at the northeasterly corner of School and Broad Streets. The wooden school was replaced with a brick building in 1955 or 1956.

The Oldtown district school float, probably prepared for the Massachusetts tercentenary parade in 1930, is parked on Bank Street. The wooden Bank Street School in the background was built about 1893. The John Woodcock School (at right) replaced the original one-room Bank Street School built about 1850 closer to Morse Street on the same lot.

Marian Gilmore's 1934 second-grade class at Bank Street School included the following, from left to right: (front row) Roland White, Marie Cilli, Carolyn Sherman, Lucille Mandalian, Jerry Fish, David McIntosh, Arthur Messier, Richard Begin, Cathy Mason, and Roselyn Gray; (middle row) Antonio Casale, Paul Auty, Jeanne Franklin, Rita Viscusi, Edna Semple, Lawrence Lincoln, Sarkis Mooradian, Earle Temple, Daniel Hunt, Myrtle Brierley, Elaine Wojciechowski, Bernice Rovelto, Marilyn Yates, Wallace Chafe, and Norman Brown; (back row) Barbara Curran, Mable Carlstrom, John Dean, Walter Dietsch, Melvin Hart, Louis Trombley, Edmund Fulton, Billy Mason, Robert Leighton, and Frankland Phipps.

The brick John Woodcock School, named after North Attleborough's first settler, designed in the English Gothic style by Boston architects McLean and Wright, was completed in 1910 by the construction firm of R.G. and J.A. Munroe. The total cost of the building, including electrical, heating, plumbing, fuel, and furnishings, was $29,460.90. The old, one-room Bank Street School was sold for $200. In 1910, it cost approximately $35 to educate a child and the average elementary-school teacher's salary was $525.

Classes of the Sacred Heart School commenced September 24, 1923. The building, facing Richards Avenue, backs up to the Sacred Heart Church on Church Street. The St. Mary's School on Broad Street also began in 1923. In 1972 the two schools combined on Broad Street and then moved to the school on Richards Avenue in 1982.

The brick grammar school, housing grades seven, eight, and nine, was named after school committee member Reverend J.D. Pierce of the Universalist Church. The interior of the building was gutted by fire on November 28, 1924. The town decided to build a junior high school addition to the high school located on South Washington Street and to remodel the J.D. Pierce School, located on Elm Street, into the new Central Fire Station.

Among the notables in this J.D. Pierce graduation photograph is Beatrice Hixon Fisher (second from the left in the back row). Beatrice was the daughter of Edgar L. Hixon (a partner in the R.F. Simmons Co.) and was the wife of Harry W. Fisher (a partner in Swift & Fisher).

Built in 1882, the second high school in North Attleborough stood at the northwest corner of High and Broad Streets until it burned on May 25, 1917.

Prior to these students attending the High Street school, high school classes commenced in 1867 in a wooden building located along South Washington, near the corner of Barrows Street. From 1833 to 1852 higher education could be attained at the North Attleborough Academy, located at the corner of North Washington and Orne Streets.

Temporarily housed in the Barrows estate, high school students eagerly watched the construction of the high school on South Washington Street until it was completed in 1920. The 1938 hurricane laid waste to the trees that stood in front of the high school and in Municipal Park (where the Barrows estate once stood).

Ronald Christianson conducts the orchestra during the dedication services of the Joseph W. Martin Jr. Elementary School in 1967.

Two
Going to Church

Built for the use of the Sunday School Society, the Cushman Union Chapel was dedicated on December 12, 1883. On July 22, 1888, the Christian Endeavor Society was formed. Horse sheds (at the right in this photograph) were erected in 1892. On November 24, 1899, the Cushman Union Congregational Society was formed and regular Sunday preaching services were inaugurated. Before 1900, services were held on an irregular basis. In 1913, the basement was transformed into a kitchen area and Sunday school room.

Being the third meetinghouse in Oldtown, the current First Congregational Church on Old Post Road was built in 1828. Ezra Walker, the builder, lived in the house almost opposite the beginning of Draper Avenue (now 382–400 Old Post Road). Trolley tracks and overhead electrical wires are visible in this photograph from about 1910.

The First Congregational Church parsonage was built during the pastorate of Reverend John Bailey, who served from 1840 to 1851. His wife, Sarah Bailey, designed the house. One of their daughters, Mrs. Mary Lincoln, was the first principal of the Boston Cooking School and authored the popular *Boston Cook Book* in 1883. In the 1920s the book continued under Fanny Farmer.

The Sacred Heart Parish was established in 1904 for the French-speaking population. Land on Church Street was purchased in 1909 from Dr. Foster and services were held in the basement starting in 1910. This view of the dedication services is looking southeast toward Richards Avenue.

Although the shell of Sacred Heart Church was completed by 1913, services continued in the basement until the interior was completed in 1929. The bell tower and steeple were removed in 1981.

The wooden First Universalist Church was dedicated on November 3, 1841. The church building was lifted and a basement and front steps added in 1865. The town clock was located in its steeple. The building was moved to Elm Street in 1882 by the Wamsutta Hotel Association and used as a hall. Town meetings were held here after the town separation in 1887.

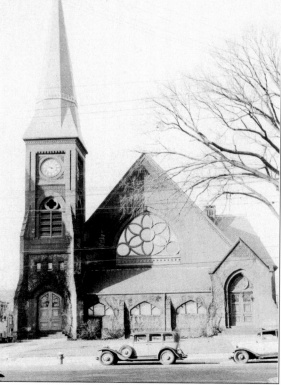

A brick church replaced the wooden church on the northerly corner of Church and North Washington Streets in 1882. The building was demolished in 1981. The rose window, among the items donated to the Royal Arts Foundation of Newport, RI, can still be enjoyed in Belmont Castle in Newport.

The Christian Union Chapel (later called the New Boston Community Chapel) was built about 1900 on New Boston Road, and was razed to make way for the Kelley Boulevard-Route 95 overpass about 1960. (Photograph courtesy of Mr. and Mrs. Jim Kenney.)

The Central Congregational Church appears to be cut out of the wilderness in this photograph taken in 1875, the year the church was completed. Actually, space for the building was cut out of the Stanley and Robinson burial ground. After securing the consent of a majority of the persons directly concerned, about 40 or 50 bodies were relocated to Mount Hope Cemetery.

Commenced in 1867, the church building at the southerly corner of East Street and North Washington Street was completed in 1870. Originally organized as the Free Evangelical Church, the group evolved into the First Methodist Episcopal Church in 1906. Most will remember this church sans the bell tower and steeple. The building was condemned in 1961 and a new church was built at Hoppin Hill Avenue.

The edifice on the southwest corner of Broad and Grove Streets, built about 1900, has housed many different church societies, including the Trinity Congregational, the First Emmanuel, the Gospel Tabernacle, and the Nazarene. The Trinity Congregational Church ran a "Chinese Sunday School" in this building from 1900 to 1910.

The parish of Grace Church was organized March 30, 1859. The wooden church building was built in 1872 and the rectory (to its left) was completed in 1873. A two-story addition to the church, the Parish House, completed in 1892, is missing from this *c.* 1884 photograph. The tower of the High Street high school is visible at the left corner of the rectory.

The wooden Grace Church and Parish House were destroyed by fire on December 2, 1929. A new stone and masonry church, incorporating the rose window and front porch from the original church, was completed in 1931. In 1957, the old rectory was moved to the southwest corner of Park and School Streets and the present rectory was built.

In this photograph, taken on May 30, 1890, the Right Reverend Matthew Harkins, Bishop of Providence, is officiating at the laying of the cornerstone of St. Mary's Church. Previous to this, services had been held in the octagon stable (at left), from the time of the purchase of the Tifft Estate in 1877.

Services continued to be held in the basement until the interior of the church was completed. A dedication service was held on December 8, 1901. The building lost some of its Gothic qualities with the lowering of the tower in 1975.

The chime of ten bells of St. Mary's Church was set up on the lawn of the round house for consecration on November 3, 1907.

This picture captured the blessing of the statue of the Virgin Mary, an annual May event. The round house served as a rectory until replaced by a brick building in 1957.

This view of North Washington Street looking north from the junction with Park Street (once part of the Old Bay Road) shows the Baptist Common as it looked in 1880. The bandstand and flagpole were erected about the time of the Civil War. The common was formed with the laying out of the Norfolk & Bristol Turnpike (North Washington Street) in 1802.

The second meetinghouse of the First Baptist Church was completed in 1817. This group gathered on the last Sunday of Reverend Wesley G. Huber's pastorate. The building was almost destroyed by fire on December 23, 1951.

Three
How to Get Around

The Rhode Island and Massachusetts Railroad, completed in 1877, connected the Providence and Worcester Railroad at Valley Falls, RI, to the New York and New England Railroad at Franklin, MA. Passenger service was available over this line from Boston to Providence. Asa Newell, pictured here, was both station agent for the railroad and postmaster (1889–1920) of the Adamsdale Post Office, which was located at the station.

In 1888–89 the Old Colony Railroad chartered the Wrentham Branch Railroad to extend to the Attleborough Branch Railroad. Later, the New York, New Haven and Hartford Railroad extended the line to connect to the Rhode Island and Massachusetts line at the Adamsdale Junction station (pictured here). The New Haven ran over this line until it was abandoned in 1963.

Having been bypassed in the 1830s, when the Boston & Providence Railroad was constructed as almost a straight shot between the two cities (running through the then much-less populated East Attleborough), the industrialists of the Falls Village and North Attleborough saw to the building of the Attleborough Branch Railroad in 1871. The Falls Village Station (pictured here) was just down the road from the home of one of the incorporators, Handel N. Daggett, and his Braid Mill (see p. 59).

The depot at the end of the line of the Attleborough Branch Railroad was located on South Washington Street about where Holbrook Avenue is today. When the inaugural train arrived, instead of arriving at the station, the train was mistakenly directed across a turntable and into the engine house. The surprised engineer couldn't find the brake lever and the engine continued through the rear wall and across the street, coming to rest on the front lawn of the home of H.F. Barrows (see p. 45), another of the incorporators.

The coal sheds and office of W.H. Riley & Son are visible behind the cars and engine facing out of the South Washington Street station at the rear of this *c.* 1873 photograph. The station was destroyed in a fire on February 10, 1893.

This view, taken from the roof of the Webster Company, shows the rails connecting to the Attleborough Branch bearing left under Broadway. This line actually bypassed the station on South Washington Street, crossing a bridge over South Washington just south of the intersection with Chestnut Street. A new station was built on Chestnut Street just before the intersection with Oak and Elm Streets. The extension of the Wrentham Branch bears to the right toward Adamsdale Junction.

The passenger station of the New York, New Haven and Hartford's Wrentham Branch line was located on Broadway between Church and High Streets. This track-side view, taken about 1910, includes the High Street bridge (at left).

This is the street-side view of the High Street station. Faced with a steadily declining number of passengers due in no small part to the increase in the use of buses and automobiles, passenger service ended in 1938.

If you arrived at the High Street station between 1913 and 1917 and wanted to put up at the Emerson House hotel, Alidor Dudley would help you with your baggage and chauffeur you to your destination. When the U.S. entered the Great War in 1917, Alidor joined the service. During his absence, the Emerson House burned and Alidor was out of a job.

This view, looking north on West Street from the junction with Broadway, was taken on August 18, 1889, and shows the construction of the railroad bridge. Note the street-level tracks and the flatbed car (at left) used to deliver the granite blocks for the bridge. Just beyond the bridge is the section of town known as Dublin (so called due its concentration of residents of Irish decent).

This c. 1900 view looking East on Elm Street includes, from left to right, the Wamsutta Stable (the old Universalist church), the Hugo Block, the junction of East Street, a residence, and the Evening Chronicle building. Note the mounted policeman (at left), the horseless carriage (believed to be that of Doctor Gerould), and the stage full of passengers, possibly part of a July Fourth parade.

The Interstate Street Railway Company's trolley line, which ran along South Washington Street from the junction with Elm Street and continued along Old Post Road and Newport Avenue on to Pawtucket, RI, began operation on December 4, 1892. This 1894 photograph shows an open trolley traveling south in front of 692 Old Post Road, just south of Mount Hope Street.

The Attleboro, North Attleboro and Wrentham Street Railway Company began service on April 5, 1890, and was acquired by the Interstate in 1893. This 1902 view shows a trolley in front of the Falls Fire Barn on Commonwealth Avenue. The line started along Elm Street in the center of town, turned right along Mount Hope Street, left onto old Commonwealth Avenue, and then right onto North Avenue into Attleborough. The New Haven was still operating the old Attleborough Branch Railroad when this photograph was taken. Note the four grade-crossing gates and the railroad passenger station (just right of center).

With the extension of the Wrentham Branch to Adamsdale, the New Haven ended its lease of the Attleborough Branch in 1903. In the same year, trolley service began along the same tracks. Electric freight service also continued, as shown here at the closed Attleborough Falls passenger station. A corner of the freight house is just visible at the far right.

With the electrification of the old Attleborough Branch, passengers had a choice of taking the original line (via street) or the new "Gee Whiz" line (via branch). The "Gee Whiz" connected with the street line near the R.F. Simmons Company on North Main Street in Attleborough. Walter Peckham and Warren Gammon are shown here in front of the line's freight motor car.

The Attleboro, North Attleboro and Wrentham Street Railway traveled along North Washington Street to Plainville. Passengers had to transfer to the Milford, Attleboro and Woonsocket Street Railway in order to reach Wrentham.

Trolley service, slowly losing passengers to competing bus lines, ended in 1932. The Interstate Transit Corporation was forced to remove the trolley tracks in 1935. The crew shown here is removing the line along North Washington Street just north of the High Street intersection.

The house at Arns' Motel (at left) is about the only thing recognizable in this view looking north along Route 1. The Route 1 bypass (the current Route 1, completed in the 1930s) would curve right just beyond the house at the right. This house stood vacant for many years until being torn down in 1997 to make way for a boat business.

A crew prepares the road surface for new cement in front of cabins along Route 1.

Four
Going to Work

The "new" E.I. Richards' building was built to take advantage of the waterpower of the Ten Mile River, which it straddled at Elm Street. The pond, which once built up behind the building and stretched from Orne Street to Fisher Street, has since been filled in by Route 1 and the old town dump. O.M. Draper, a manufacturer of rolled plate, fire-gilt, and nickel chains, occupied the first floor of the building when this *c.* 1876 photograph was taken. F.B. Richards & Co., known as E. Ira Richards & Co. in New York City (where many of the jewelry firms of the period had offices), manufactured rolled gold-plated bracelets, bangles, and novelties on the second floor. This firm traced its history back to 1833 at this same site. H.D. Merritt & Co., a manufacturer of rolled plate and silver chains, occupied the third floor.

By 1907, when this photograph was taken, E.I. Richards's buildings were known as the Company Shops and included the "new" building (at left, sans the top two floors of the towers shown in the previous picture), the older building (at right), and other buildings behind both. Among the jewelry manufactures located here were T.G. Frothingham, A.L. Lindroth, Swift & Fisher, J.P. Bonnett and Cheever, and Tweedy & Co. The Handy & Harman building stands in front of these buildings at the northeast corner of Elm and East Washington Streets.

This was the home of E. Ira Richards. The Tweedy family later owned this house and the factories the Richards owned across Elm Street. The house and its 6-acre estate were sold in 1963 after the death of Mrs. Maude Tweedy. The impressive home was torn down to make room for the First National Store plaza, which is now home to Ocean Fresh Seafood.

This house at 64 High Street was built in 1878 for Oscar M. Draper. Mister Draper started in the jewelry business in 1862 under the name of O.M. Draper & Co. E.I. Richards was the "& Co." The firm was best known for its chains, but after his death in 1890, ladies bracelets were added to their line. The LeStage Mfg. Co. is a descendant of this company. (Photograph courtesy of Attleboro Industrial Museum.)

The brick jewelry factory and house of William H. Robinson was located on the westerly side of Old Post Road south of Draper Avenue. W.H. Robinson acquired the house in 1837 and shortly thereafter built the brick factory. Here he manufactured high quality, solid gold jewelry and was succeeded in business by his son Daniel. Both buildings were razed to make way for Route 295 in 1965.

This was the home of Willard Robinson, who pioneered the manufacture of gilt buttons in the United States in 1826 at Attleborough Falls. In 1812 his father, Colonel Obed Robinson, and uncle, Otis Robinson, started the first button factory in the United States, also at Attleborough Falls. (An 1890s photograph, courtesy of the Attleboro Industrial Museum.)

In 1873 Robert F. Simmons' career, manufacturing rolled plated chains, started in this building on East Street, opposite Bruce Avenue. In 1874, partnered with Edgar L. Hixon, R.F. Simmons & Co. moved to a building on Mt. Hope Street, just south of Daggett's Braid Mill (see p. 59). In 1876 they moved to the Freeman factory on Robinson Avenue and then to a new factory on North Main Street in Attleborough in 1893.

The H.F. Barrows estate, pictured about 1880, included all of the land of Municipal Park, the town pool, and the town hall. This building was used for high school classes in 1918–20 (see p. 20).

The H.F. Barrows Co. has occupied this building at the northeast corner of South Washington and Chestnut Streets since it was constructed in 1907. H.F. Barrows began manufacturing jewelry in 1853 in a factory just south of the braid mill on Mt. Hope Street, moved to the Richards' building in 1856, and moved to the "Beehive" (now apartments) at the northeast corner of Division and Broad Streets about 1862.

A fire struck the Robinson Avenue factory of B.S. Freeman & Co. on March 27, 1901. In 1846, Benjamin and his brother Joseph started manufacturing rings in a small shop next to their father's home on Mt. Hope Street. In 1850 the factory south of the braid mill (see p. 59) was built for them and they started manufacturing rolled plated chains. In 1858 they moved to Robinson Avenue.

The home Benjamin Stanley Freeman, built about 1856 at 390 Mount Hope Street, is at or about the location of his father's home and B.S. Freeman's first shop. Despite the removal of some of the ornamentation shown in this c. 1900 photograph, the house (now an apartment house) is still easily recognizable today.

Fire destroyed the South Bulfinch Street factory of J.F. Sturdy & Co. about 1900. The rear of the Gold Medal Braid Co. appears in the background. The Sturdy brothers, J.F. and J.H., discovered the process of making rolled gold-plated stock while in Providence and introduced it in Attleborough Falls in 1849. After the fire, the firm moved to the Freeman factories on Robinson Avenue.

The Robinson Avenue factories included, from left to right, D. Evans & Co. (buttons), R.F. Simmons & Co. (gold chains), B.S. Freeman (gold chains), and various other smaller jewelry manufacturers. D. Evans & Co. succeeded the Robinsons (see p. 44) and manufactured plain, fancy, military, gilt, and silver-plated buttons starting in 1848. (An 1890s photograph, courtesy of the Attleboro Industrial Museum.)

The V.H. Blackinton & Co. building, built in 1869, is at right in this *c.* 1900 view looking north on Commonwealth Avenue at Simmons' Park. The firm started in business in 1857 in the Robinsonville School.

This 1902 V.H. Blackinton & Co. photograph includes, from left to right, George Metters, Harry S. Wilmarth, James Dow, Artie Boyce, Bill Joyce, Jack Glancy, Mr. Hoddie, Ed Shepardson, Barney Logan, Tommy Franklin, and Gus Cahoon.

The Robinsonville School bell (shown in the cupola of the V.H. Blackinton & Co. building in this 1968 photograph) and the eagle weathervane were given to the Falls Fire Barn Museum when the firm moved to the Industrial Park.

This 1951 V.H. Blackinton & Co. photograph includes, from left to right, Ronald Precourt, Jean Mason, Thelma Cunningham, and Bob Langille. The company remains one of the oldest and largest manufacturers of society, military, fire, and police badges, medals, and souvenirs.

This was the residence of Theron I. Smith. T.I. Smith manufactured jewelry with various partners in various locations starting in 1860. By 1890, T.I. Smith & Co. was considered one of the largest firms in North Attleborough. This house was removed to make way for the Hotel Hixon, now the Madonna Manor.

By 1903, T.I. Smith & Co. occupied their new building on South Washington Street, across from Chestnut Street. They manufactured collar buttons, scarf pins, studs, bracelets, and pearl goods at this location. The building was later the home of Commercial Press and currently is occupied by Jeweled Cross Co. Inc.

This 1907 postcard depicts the Riley & French Factory on Broad Street opposite Tifft Street. In 1913 the building housed the following firms: C. Ray Randall & Co. (gold-filled and sterling jewelry), Riley & French (jewelry jobbers), the W. & S. Blackinton Co. (gold-filled chains), and G.C. Hudson & Co. (gold plated and sterling jewelry). Alton H. Riley and G. Herbert French had a financial interest in all of these firms.

This photograph of A.H. Bliss & Co. employees was probably taken about the time of the business's establishment in 1888 when it occupied the factory on Broad Street opposite Tifft. By 1903 the chain manufacturer had moved to the Whitney building on Chestnut Street (see p. 53).

In 1913, this factory at the northwest corner of Bruce Avenue and East Street housed the following businesses: C.K. Grouse Co. (class and fraternity pins, medals, rings, and lockets); Straker & Freeman (designers, hub and die cutters, jewelers tools, die forgers, and blacksmiths); and C.E. Sandland & Son (enameling and engine turning).

This 1910 view depicts the residence of Louis E. Freeman at 206 South Washington Street. Mister Freeman was the partner of Herbert J. Straker in the firm of Straker & Freeman. In 1913 he purchased the F.H. Cutler Co., manufacturer of 10k gold broaches, bracelets, hatpins, and lockets at the Manufacturers Building (see p. 53).

Originally the Whitney Building, this Chestnut Street factory building has also been called (depending on the tenant) the Bliss Building, the Doran & Bagnall Building, the Bugbee & Niles Building, and the Standard Chain Building. F.G. Whitney & Co., a manufacturer of inexpensive jewelry, built the factory here in 1876. The original building burned and was almost immediately rebuilt. (An 1890s photograph, courtesy of the Attleboro Industrial Museum.)

The Manufacturers' Building, built in 1906, housed the O.M. Draper Co., the LeStage Mfg. Co., the Mandalian Mfg. Co., the L.S. Peterson Co., Swift & Fisher, and the White Mfg. Co. Inc. when this c. 1940 photograph was taken. Mandalian's Lustre Pearl enameled metal-mesh purses are highly collectible today. The building was renovated into the retail and office space of Tower Square in 1985.

The Totten Building on East Street had been purchased and occupied by J.J. Sommer & Co. when this 1905 photograph was taken. By the late 1920s, the Evans Case Co. occupied its entirety and soon saw the need to expand it. Compacts, lighters, cigarette cases, and evening bags were their best-known products, but their diverse line even included fishing lures. The firm, which had once been North Attleborough's largest employer, closed in 1960. The buildings were taken over by L.G. Balfour in 1961.

The familiar two-story addition and its familiar Madonna sculpture had not been added when this photograph of the Creed Rosary Co. was taken. William J. Creed, who had been a salesman for Jeweled Cross Co. of North Attleborough, started this firm about 1946.

The H.W. Tufts Tool Co., one of a group of supporting firms required by the jewelry manufacturers, was located at 77 Elm Street when this photograph was taken in 1930. A corner of the Adeline Apartments (later Miner's Furniture Store) is just visible at right. Harry W. Tufts was fire chief when the Emerson House burned (see p. 90).

The Mason Box Company, another of the firms that the jewelry industry spawned, began manufacturing jewelers cards, boxes, and bags in a barn in back of the founders' home on Mount Hope Street in 1891. This c. 1915 photograph shows the peaked-roof factory (built about 1900) and later extensions accounting to a growing business. Many generations of the same families have given this firm a stable and loyal work force.

The factories on Broad Street at Whiting were occupied by R. Blackinton & Co. (sterling and 14k gold novelties), F.M. Whiting & Co. (sterling silver table and hollow ware), the Mason Lenzen Co., J.O. Copeland & Co., and Sturtevant & Whiting in this 1913 view. Blackinton started manufacturing solid and plated gold jewelry in 1863. Frank Whiting took over the factory vacated when his father's company moved to New York City in 1876.

W.D. Whiting started in the jewelry business with Albert Tifft in 1840. His estate at Park Street, about where Adams Street is today, exhibited the opulence of the man who grew the "standard silverware" manufactory he started on Broad Street in 1866 into an internationally known concern. The solarium (at left) is now part of Johnny's Oil on South Street in Plainville.

G.K. Webster started in the manufacture of plated jewelry in 1880 at the Company Shops (see p. 42). The Webster Company moved to its new building along the railroad tracks on Broadway at the top of Bank Street about 1903. Here they manufactured a line of sterling novelties, tableware, and toilet goods. Within ten years, a three-story addition along Broadway, not shown in this 1906 photograph, was necessary.

THE WEBSTER COMPANY VENERABLES
Charter Dinner — Colonial Inn, Plainville, Massachusetts
June 21, 1951

1. J. Edward Costigan (43)	11. Henry Boerger (38)	21. William Collins (34)	31. Harold Armstrong (28)	41. Robert Gay (30)
2. Raymond McGettrick (35)	12. Dona Desilets (35)	22. Harold Lewis (35)	32. Harold Phillips (46)	42. Frederick Negus (37)
3. John Desilets (45)	13. Rhoda White (39)	23. Gerald Riley (Guest)	33. Howard Bigelow (37)	43. Russell Scott (Guest)
4. Edwin Newcomb (45)	14. Annie Metcalf (45)	24. Carl Beresford (34)	34. Elmer Cobb (41)	44. Sayward Farnum (Guest)
5. William Robbins (47)	15. Bessie Rhodes (29)	25. John Cullen (50)	35. Ezekiel Irving (39)	45. Eugene Fournier (47)
6. Harry Cumberland (49)	16. Mary Kiernan (37)	26. Thomas Perry (48)	36. Ethel Rhodes (38)	46. Benjamin Armstrong (48)
7. William Hoyle (36)	17. Grace Blanchard (45)	27. Thomas LeBlanc (32)	37. Paul Cornish (33)	47. Arthur Ashworth (Guest)
8. Harold Anderson (38)	18. Martha White (51)	28. William Robinson (49)	38. Alfred Willmore (29)	48. Chester Caswell (38)
9. Arthur Abells (47)	19. Lester Welch (41)	29. Allan Caswell (25)	39. Robert Allen (48)	49. Sinclair Weeks (Guest)
10. William Swedberg (38)	20. Warren Pierce (47)	30. Herbert Follett (46)	40. Arthur Greene (47)	

Members not present for photograph

William Burke (49)
Arthur Fournier (33)
Donat Fournier (32)
Arthur LeBlanc (28)
W. Everett White (49)

Number in parentheses to right of name denotes years of accumulated service

The firm of Paye & Baker Mfg. Co. started as Simmons & Paye in Providence, RI, in 1897. The name changed with a change in partnerships in 1900 and the firm moved in 1903 to this factory along the southerly side of Richards Avenue near the intersection of Broadway. Frank L. Baker and Paye family members Charles T. (partner), Arthur (clerk), Frederick (foreman), and Harry (die cutter) all followed the firm to North Attleborough and lived within walking distances of the factory.

This is a rear view of the Paye & Baker Mfg. Co. in 1912. The firm manufactured fancy flatware, souvenir spoons, hatpins, sterling jewelry, silver photo frames, and linked chain, metal-mesh bags. In the 1950s, the firm became a division of the Bishop Company, which eventually moved their eyeglass frame manufactory here.

This dam, built in 1831 at a natural falls on the Ten Mile River (hence the village's name), created the Falls Pond reservoir. The dam controlled the flow of water that powered the mills at Attleborough Falls. (An 1890s photograph, courtesy of the Attleboro Industrial Museum.)

This is H.N. Daggett's Gold Medal Braid Co. along Mt. Hope Street, just south of South Bulfinch Street, as it looked in 1880. The largest building was built in 1857 by H.M. Richards for an ill-fated jewelry venture and then reacquired by Daggett for his manufactory of dress braids, coat bindings, and fish lines. The three-story building is that built for the Freeman Brothers (see p. 46).

From his house on the hill near the corner of Elm and Mt. Hope Streets, H.N. Daggett had a good view of his braid mill and of the trains of the railroad line he helped establish (see p. 32). After his death in 1894, the braid mill continued as the Standard Braid Co., and then as the International Braid Co. until 1941. The house was torn down in 1935.

The C. Ray Randall Co., established in 1901 at the Riley and French Building (see p. 51), manufactured gold-filled and sterling jewelry. In 1940 the firm moved to the newly vacant braid mill building (see p. 59) and manufactured jewelry for such firms as Sarah Coventry, Coro, and Trifari. In 1965, they even made pins depicting The Beatles. This is Mr. Randall's High Street home; it later became the home of Jarvis Hunt (see p. 112).

The Royal Textile Co. (a small concern that lasted for only a few years) manufactured shoelaces here when this *c.* 1907 photograph was taken. Later the building was the home of Maintien Bros. Inc. and the Newell Mfg. Co., jewelry manufacturers. It was located about where the parking for Oldham Electric is today.

This view looking north on Mendon Road, just before Cushman Road, shows the third Adamsdale mill (built in 1882) on this site along Abbott Run. The first cotton mill was built about 1826. The first and second mills burned. The City of Pawtucket removed the mill in 1926 when it bought much of Adamsdale for a proposed, but never built, reservoir. (A 1914 photograph, courtesy of the North Attleborough Historical Society.)

Formed in 1881, W.G. Clark & Co. manufactured sleeve buttons. About 1908, the firm moved from the Totten Building (see p. 87) to this building built for them on Chestnut Street at the corner of what was then Jefferson Street (before the construction of Route 1). In the late 1920s the firm changed its name to the Clark Lighter Co. By 1933, the building was vacant.

Noah J. Magnan established his building and contracting business at Dexter Street in 1890 and by 1903 he was advertising lumber and building materials. By 1917, he manufactured tennis racquets on Dexter Street and turned to them exclusively after his lumberyard burned on July 2, 1922. His racquets became world-renowned and the firm continued manufacturing them into the 1960s.

Five
Going to Shop

This photograph and the next three photographs illustrate the main business section of North Attleborough at the turn of the century. Starting here, looking north on South Washington Street (just south of the Bank Street intersection), we have the following: (at left) the Bank Building (Glaiel Block), the International House (hotel), and the trolley car waiting room and confectioners; (at right) Cornell's Paint Store and Badaracco's Fruit Store. The building that housed the waiting room was later moved around the corner onto Richards Avenue. The Cornell building was moved across South Washington Street to the corner of Richards Avenue and housed Degrenia's Cafe. The Attleboro Trust Co. purchased the Cornell building in 1966 and tore it down for additional bank parking.

Continuing north on North Washington Street from the center of town, we have the following: (at left) the Hancock Building, the Boyle or Burt Block (Vigorito's), the Anawan Block, and the Odd Fellows Building; (at right) the Wamsutta House (two buildings), Barrows' Block (closer to street), the Academy Building (moved here from the corner of Orne Street—see p. 19), and the Masonic Building.

Looking back south on North Washington Street from just north of Orne Street, we have the following: (at left) Codding's Block, Orne Street, Kendall's Block, and the Masonic Building; (at right) Church Street, the Odd Fellows Building, the Anawan Block, and the Boyle Block.

Continuing north on North Washington Street, just north of Orne Street, we have the following: (at left) the Attleborough Savings Bank, Hall's Block (Schofield's), Guild's Block, High Street, and the Ralston Block; (at right) Pearson & Bloomer's Cash Market and Kostas Kouyas & Co. fruit stand.

The operators of the telephone exchange, located in the brick building at 38 South Washington Street (just south of the post office), were a busy bunch until dial telephone service was introduced into town in 1955. The Providence Telephone Company of Massachusetts provided service until absorbed into New England Telephone System.

This is the Bank Building on the corner of South Washington and Bank Streets as it looked about 1880. It housed the North Attleborough National Bank, the Attleborough Savings Bank, the law offices of Joseph E. Pond Jr. (a solicitor of patents), and a meat market.

This is David Badaracco's fruit and confectionery store as it looked about 1905. From left to right are David Badaracco, August Badaracco, Jesse B. Stevens, and Ted Desjardins. Police officer Jesse B. Stevens wore badge #1 and Hotel Corner was his beat. Jesse was on the force for many years and shows up on many postcard views of the center of town. (Photograph courtesy of the North Attleborough Historical Society.)

This is the Badaracco Block at the southeast corner of South Washington and Elm Streets as it looked in 1915. It replaced the wooden building that housed Badaracco's fruit store. Edward J. Kivlin's Drug Store gave way to a succession of other druggists including Fisk's, Brennan's, and Bernier's. Some may call this the Abizaid building after Sadie Abizaid, who owned the building in the 1980s.

This is the center of town, looking north on North Washington, in 1921. The one-story Brown Block (at right) replaced the Emerson Hotel (the Wamsutta House—see p. 89), which burned in 1918. Thomas F. Coady ran Wamsutta Drug in the corner shop of the Brown Block. The three-story Barrows' Block survived the fire.

Edwin Hancock stands next to his delivery wagon along the Richards Avenue side of his store in the Hancock Building (see p. 64) about 1907. Edwin continued the family grocery business his grandfather, Timothy E. Hancock, and father, George Hancock, ran at the same location. The building was erected in 1859 by Ira Conant, who ran a dry goods business and hoopskirt manufactory here. Druggist F.H. Gould occupied the other storefront in this building.

Martin Jensen ran the Jensen Motor Co. at 41 Richards Avenue in the 1920s through the 1950s. In 1940 he advertised that he sold approved DeSoto-Chrysler parts and that service was provided by factory-trained mechanics using the most modern equipment. Gaudette Leather Goods, Inc. presently occupies the building.

Technician Al Houde (at left) and owner Albert E. "Bud" Tongue pose in the repair room of Tongue TV Sales & Service. Bud's store was located in the right-hand storefront of the Hancock Building (see p. 64) in the 1950s.

The Bay State Tea & Butter Company store of A.B. Cook and H.E. White looked much like this when it opened in the Anawan Block (see p. 64) in 1901. By 1913, their stores could also be found in Whitman, Rockland, Norwood, Athol, Gardner, Mansfield, Ware, and Greenfield. They offered the best in butter, cheese, eggs, tea, and coffee.

This is a portion of the Wamsutta House, along North Washington Street, about 1890. A.L. Audrain was a manufacturers' agent and jobber of fine Havana cigars. The Opera House door (at left) led to a hall with a seating capacity of eight hundred. The balcony over this storefront was used for band concerts.

Edward A. Lavery and Joseph Irvine opened their liquor store in the Barrows' Block soon after prohibition ended. The Barrows' Block was moved from one side of the Brown Block on North Washington Street to the other side of it on Elm Street (see p. 67). The two men are seen here cleaning up after the 1938 hurricane. The building that had escaped the hotel fire was destroyed by a fire of its own on March 25, 1939.

Linley's Service Station moved to this location at the northwest corner of Elm and East Streets from their station on the corner of Barrows and South Washington Streets in the late 1920s. Linley's advertised as the town's only complete, one-stop service station. They also sold fuel and range oils. From left to right are an unidentified man, Luigi Hevey, Walter Burlingame, and Irving Linley in 1938.

Nahum Perry & Co., a hardware store, was located in the Barrows' Block (see p. 64). The storefront is shown here decorated at around the time of President McKinley's assassination in 1901. The products on display, including the fruit pickers (at left), reflect a time when agriculture was still an important industry in town.

Businesses in this pre-1880 photograph of the Kendall Block (see p. 64) included F.A. Sheldon (druggist), the Boston Store (clothing), the post office, the Attleboro Chronicle Printing Office, F.L. Burden (M.D.), and J. Blaisdell (dentist). The Providence Telephone Exchange's original location was on the second floor of this building. They had one room and less than three hundred subscribers.

The J.J. Newberry Co. moved into this block at the southerly corner of Orne and North Washington Streets in 1930 and was a fixture along the main street for about 50 years. The toy department in the basement, with the gum machine strategically located at the bottom of the stairs, was always a child's first destination. (A 1968 photograph, courtesy of Alan Bliek.)

Leon W. Briggs stands in the doorway of the North Attleboro Cash Grocery he ran with Charles E. Steele. The store was located in the southernmost storefront of the Boyle Block (see p. 64) when this *c.* 1907 photograph was taken.

The interior of the Attleborough Savings Bank was newly refurbished when this photograph, staged with employees on both sides of the counter, was taken in 1953. From left to right are as follows: (customer side) Doris Jordan, Adele Miller, Lila Hang (partially hidden), Gertrude Gamble, and Albert Totten; (teller side) Norma Patton, June Jenckes, Alice Swedberg, Elsie Lightfoot, and Dot Henshaw.

The Guild Block, pictured about 1890, was located at the southerly corner of High and North Washington Streets. In 1890, the store fronts housed, from left to right, Wm. M. Hall (stove dealer and locksmith), Miss Harriet Bonney (milliner), W. Fisk (harness maker), and Arthur S. Bishop (furniture dealer). The block burned and is now the site of the Pace Building.

The Barden Bros. Clothing Store float is shown in a Fourth of July parade about 1910. The background is the westerly side of North Washington Street, just north of High Street. The Ralston Block at the corner of High Street had not yet been extended north to Capadanno's store. The High Street high school tower is visible over the float.

Herbert T. Scott, seen here about 1913, ran a grocery store in the DeBlois Block on North Washington Street, just south of Fisher Street. Mr. Scott always had a large black cat sleeping in a chair by his stove (hidden by the seed packet display at center).

Charles Ralston and his sister Ethel stand in the doorway of his Brick Oven Bakery on North Washington Street in 1904. The wagon driver at right is Ed McNeil from Plainville. The baker at left is Pat Smith. The one-story building left of the bakery was Capodanno's Fruit Store. Capodanno's added liquors after Prohibition ended.

Robert C. Moulton, seen here behind the counter about 1933, managed the First National Store at 114 Park Street. In 1933, besides this store on Park Street, there were three other First National Stores on North Washington Street and yet another on Elm Street. Not to be out done, there were four A&P Grocery Stores, one at Park and West Streets and three on North Washington Street. There were also a number of independent grocers.

In the days before Budweiser used Clydesdales, mules pulled the beer wagon past the North End Social Club on North Washington Street in 1954. Joseph Nolan started the business here in the late 1930s. (Photograph courtesy of Bob Oldham.)

This was the Sweetland Farm when this photograph was taken in the 1870s. Some time after the Landry family purchased the farm at 91 Paine Road, the stone wall was taken to Morse Sand & Gravel and crushed. (Photograph courtesy of the Landry family.)

This is the farm of Albert L. Allen on the westerly side of Allen Avenue about 1900. Albert manufactured cider and vinegar here. Prior to 1900, Henry K.W. Allen ran the Attleboro Vineyard, possibly at the same location, and advertised unfermented wine for the sacrament and pure native wines for medicinal use. His wine was awarded the Silver Medal for its purity and excellence as an unfermented sacramental wine at the Farmers and Mechanics Association Fair (see p. 118) in October 1883.

This is the Halliday Farm on the southerly side of Holmes Road, at the Rhode Island state line, as it looked in 1938. The Halliday's raised up to 500 hogs at a time as well as 25 dairy cows and 200 hens. Eggs were traded for groceries at the market. Home delivery of milk was tried for a short time, until the hired hand was caught keeping all the proceeds. Later they sold their milk to Ray Jenkes, who delivered Cloverleaf Dairy milk in glass bottles. (Photograph courtesy of Robert Halliday Jr.)

This is the Sayles Dairy Farm on Ellis Road, at High Street, as it looked soon after Arthur Evans purchased it in the late 1930s. Millen T. Sayles and his wife, Millie, ran the dairy here since the early 1900s. If you attended North Attleborough schools in the 1940s or '50s, you probably remember their milk bottles with the cow's face on front. (Photograph courtesy of Ervin and Lovis Estey.)

In the days before electric refrigeration, most of North Attleborough's homes and stores relied upon ice harvested from either Whiting's Pond or Todd's Pond (depicted here). By the time this 1906 photograph was taken, farmers George, Henry, James, and William Todd found selling ice more profitable than farming and founded the Oldtown Ice Co. Todd's Pond was located on the westerly side of Old Post Road near the corner of Allen Avenue. The Oldtown Church is visible in the background.

One of the Oldtown Ice wagons makes a delivery to William Sharp's Confectionery store, the left-most storefront in Kendall's Block (see p. 64), about 1915. Note the MOXIE sign.

This is the Rioux Ice Co. icehouse on Whiting's Pond at the bend of Moran Street in the 1920s. On the wagons, from left to right, are Ray Bishop, Joe McCretton, John McCormack, Louis Clancy, Charles Russell, and Howard Rioux. Jack Nichols stands by the Oldsmobile at right. Raoul Jeanneau is on the ladder. Owner John Rioux stands at the open doorway.

The Attleboro Coal Co. delivers coal down the chute into the basement of Schofield Hardware in the early 1940s. In the Guild Block, from left to right, are Eugene Hamel (barber pole), the Oaks Dairy Kitchen (see p. 94), Aubin's Ladie's Clothing, the Ann-Marie Dress Shop, Golomboski Shoes, Electric Shoe Re-Soling, Railway Express, and Jack & Harry's Auto Store.

Driver Thomas Rooney delivers a load of coal to the Chestnut Street yard of W.H. Riley & Son. Marcus Ralston, treasurer of the company, is at right. The other gentleman is unidentified. The Union Power/Barber Electric building is visible over the trailer.

Cargill's grain elevator and lumberyard and the Union Power Building were located just east of the Attleborough Branch Railroad station. The Union Power Building housed a number of jewelry firms when this photograph was taken about 1910. The Union Power Building, then the home of the Barber Electric Company, burned in 1953 and was replaced by the present one-story building on the northeast corner of East and Chestnut Streets in 1954.

This was the home of Henry A. Guild, the bearded gentleman in the well house, and the Henry H. Clark grocery store about 1900. The store was located on the easterly side of May Street, just south of the Adamsdale Mill and the Abbott Run.

Delphis Plante stands in front of the Farmers Market he ran and the pumps of Eugene Plante's Sunoco gas station on the easterly side of South Washington, near the top of Red Rock Hill. The location was approximately where Toys R Us is today. At various times Delphis also owned and operated the Juiceland Store on Route 1, a market on Richards Avenue, and another on Commonwealth Avenue. Delphis died at the age of 99 in 1993. (A 1933 photograph, courtesy of Sandra Plante Burlingame.)

This is the Broadway Market of Ernest Hebert in the 1970s. Besides newspapers, groceries, and penny candy, Mr. Hebert was always ready to serve up political and social commentary. This was just one of the many "neighborhood markets" that once dotted North Attleborough. How many do you remember? (Photograph courtesy of Gilberte Hebert.)

The Budweiser Beer wagon also visited Stevens' Market in 1954. Richard "Dick" Stevens stands in front of his store on Smith Street at the southwest corner of Fisher Street. His home is to the left of the store.

The Evening Chronicle Building, pictured in 1906, was located on Elm Street where Tower Square now stands. The tower of the Richards' Building (see p. 41) is visible at right. The newspaper, established in 1870, moved to Church Street in 1907. Residents of this period turned to this newspaper, about half of its space taken by ads, to find out what the merchants were selling.

Tony LaFratta stands in front of his grocery store at 325 Chestnut Street. The store was strategically situated next to the Mt. Hope Street School; children can be seen in its play-yard to the far left of the photograph. The store currently houses Homespun Antiques. (A 1920s photograph, courtesy of Theresa LaFratta Bunker.)

The "via street" trolley heads south on Mt. Hope Street, soon to take a right onto Commonwealth Avenue between the store and water trough at right. When this c. 1910 photograph was taken, Oscar Newell ran his grocery store in the building on the northeast corner of Commonwealth Avenue and Mt. Hope Street. Edward Rockett's barbershop was located in the building at left, behind the horse, on Mt. Hope Street, which was later home to Diamond's Cafe.

The dry goods store owned by Joseph Endres was located in the building at the right in this c. 1910 photograph looking west on Commonwealth Avenue from in front of the Falls Fire Station. George Chadwick's Attleborough Falls News Bureau was located in the building at the left.

David Matthew probably did not have a self-service island at Matthew's Garage at 160 Commonwealth Avenue, but Jean Mason serves some up for Edna Semple while Cathy Mason watches. Peter Gorney's grocery store, later the Sugar & Spice Pastry Shop, is in the background of this 1944 photograph.

Standing in front of Mrs. Alma Kenney's variety store in the late 1940s are, from left to right, Patty Semple (the sister of Mrs. Kenney's daughter-in-law Edna), and Mrs. Kenney's grandchildren, Dottie Roberts and Mike Griswold. The store was located on the easterly side of New Boston Road, now Kelley Boulevard, near the current intersection with Landry Avenue.

Six
Sleep and Eat in Town

Newell's Tavern, built in 1761 and pictured here as it looked in 1894, was located on the easterly side of Old Post Road, just south of Stagecoach Road. On a map of Attleborough in 1832, it still shows up as S. Newell's Inn. By 1895, the property had been acquired by the Todd family and others and soon was a multi-family dwelling. The building was eventually torn down.

The Hatch House burned January 20, 1893, and was torn down in August of 1893. Israel Hatch built the Steamboat Hotel in 1806 and ran it as an inn on the Norfolk and Bristol Turnpike, which he had a part in seeing constructed. The inn, which stood on North Washington Street, just north of the Historical Society property, was converted into tenements about 1840. The fire started in a room used as the shoe shop of Tom Jordan.

This Daggett homestead, built by Ebenezer Daggett on the East Bay Road in 1721, was run as the Rose and Crown Tavern from 1725 to 1788. Five generations of the Daggett family lived here, including four Revolutionary War veterans. The house was located on the easterly side of Kelley Boulevard, between the old intersection with Towne Street and the intersection with Bungay Road.

The Wamsutta House, located at the northeast corner of North Washington and Elm Streets, opened March 1, 1872. This hotel replaced another, the Union House, which was built in 1860 and burned in 1870. Business was such that an addition, not shown in this 1870s photograph, was made, extending another block down Elm Street at right.

By 1907, Frank O. Emerson operated the Wamsutta House and renamed it the Emerson House. The hotel had 75 rooms, including private suites with baths, a large dining hall, and an opera house. The building was home to many other businesses and the post office. Frank also ran Emerson's Cafe in the Bates Building in the center of Attleboro. Alex Emerson was proprietor of the Plainville Public Market, most recently known as Falk's Market.

About 5 p.m. on January 3, 1918, a fire started in the Emerson House laundry. Firemen from Attleboro, North Attleborough, Pawtucket, and Central Falls battled the blaze all evening and into the next day. They managed to prevent the fire from spreading to the rest of the business district and slowed the fire enough so that many guests and stores were able to rescue their stocks, but the hotel was a complete loss. This view looks southeast from North Washington Street toward the Badaracco building.

The town was without a hotel until the Hotel Hixon opened in April of 1928. In this photograph taken September 13, 1930, a viewing stand has been set up in front of the hotel and a crowd has gathered to watch the Massachusetts Tercentenary Parade. Never very successful, the hotel was purchased by the Catholic Diocese of Fall River in 1962 and Madonna Manor opened in 1966.

This 1950s aerial view depicts Fox's Tourist Court on Route 1 at Quinn Street. The lighthouse (next to the driveway at right) was a familiar landmark on Route 1 from the time George Farrand constructed his Lighthouse Cabins about 1940. After Fox's, the cabins were known as the Abbey Motel. The lighthouse and cabins were removed in the 1980s when John E. Daly built the two-story A'Rann Motor Inn.

Bunny Bonin's Cabins on the westerly side of Route 1 at Draper Avenue were another of the cabin-style motels to spring up on Route 1 in the 1940s. The signage out front attempted to attract business away from the competition. The cabins were removed to make way for the re-routing of Draper Avenue in the 1960s. Some were sold to individuals, including two that were used to keep pigs. The pigs tore up the linoleum and $50 was found.

Cooper's Cabins and Garage, built about 1930 and depicted here in 1938, were located on the easterly side of Route 1, north of Draper Avenue, before Draper was re-routed. In the 1940s, William Keefe bought the cabins and renamed them Bill's Bay State Cabins.

Arns' Restaurant and Hotel Cottages, depicted here in the 1940s, were located on the easterly side of Route 1 just south of Old Post Road. Their gas station and more cottages were located across Route 1. The cabins shown here are gone, but the restaurant building was moved southeast on the lot to make way for a Lum's Restaurant and is currently occupied by the Nantucket Deli.

CLUB HUMMOCKS

BOSTON ROAD ~ NO. ATTLEBORO, MASS.

Exceptional Entertainment   "**THE RENDEVOUS OF THE SMART SET**"   PHONE 20124

In 1917, Oscar Clairville ran the LeChateau Hotel on Route 1. Oscar ran foul of the law for serving alcohol and LeChateau was taken for taxes in 1924. In the late 1920s and early 1930s, Henry Johnson of Providence ran Ye Old Hummocks in the same location. Here he added live entertainment and advertised as Club Hummocks to attract the "flapper" crowd.

Edwin A. Robinson, a jewelry manufacturer in Attleborough and the son of William H. Robinson (see p. 43), built this house about 1880. The house, shown here in 1894, was located on the westerly side of South Washington Street, about where Route 295 crosses today. After it became a restaurant, a large, one-story addition was made to the right of the house. About 1935 Edmund Dreyfus purchased Ye Old Hummocks and renamed it LeChateau Dreyfus. LeChateau Dreyfus burned on April 9, 1948.

Abiel Codding, president of the Attleborough Savings Bank and the North Attleborough Gas Light Company, owned this house on Elm Street (depicted here in 1890). After Abiel's death in 1901, various members of the Lavery family owned the house. In 1948, Ori Scarlatelli and Jack Ippolito opened the Brook Manor Restaurant here. The Brook Manor, expanded over the years, has always offered some of the most elegant dining experiences between Boston and Providence.

This photograph of the Oaks Dairy Kitchen, tearoom and confectioners, was taken in the summer of 1938. Lloyd W. Hang (at left) was the manager. Lloyd's wife, Lila (Scott) Hang, is at center. The woman behind the counter is not identified. The enterprise was located in the Guild Block on North Washington Street (see p. 80).

The Red Rock Hill Diner was originally Mancini's Service Diner, installed in Providence, RI, in 1946. The diner was moved to Plainville, where it became Don's Diner. Don's Diner was moved to the pictured location on July 2, 1969. Don's new diner, the former Minute Man Diner on Route 1 in North Attleborough, was installed on July 8, 1969. The Red Rock Hill Diner, moved in 1987 to make way for the re-routing of Allen Avenue and the Emerald Square Mall, is now the Bolton Service Diner in Bolton's Landing, NY.

Howard Johnson's familiar orange roof was a longtime landmark on Route 1 at the junction of South Washington Street. HoJo's offered a place to unwind after a late movie or evening of dancing. In the late 1980s, CVS plaza replaced this building, which itself had replaced a wooden Howard Johnson's, the second restaurant in the HoJo's chain.

The Log Cabin, pictured in 1930, was located on Route 1 at the bottom of Elmwood Street. The Cargill family operated the restaurant and lived in the first house on the northerly side of Elmwood, which can be seen just behind the right corner of the restaurant. Later Tom Shaunessy ran it before it was removed for Joe Jakuboski's Dairy Queen. The Flower Studio moved to the site when Dairy Queen built a new building to the north.

This is how the Sayles Dairy Farms' Ice Cream and Milk Bar looked when it opened in 1940. It had the perfect location, directly opposite the high school on South Washington Street. Primarily window service, it also had a few stools inside for counter service. (Photograph courtesy of Ervin and Lovis Estey.)

Mabel Evans (left), the wife of Arthur (see p. 78), operated the Sayles Dairy Farms' Ice Cream and Milk Bar. If you ate here in the 1950s, you are sure to remember Minnie Wakefield, the redheaded waitress, and probably enjoyed an ice cream sundae like the one she holds here. (Photograph courtesy of Ervin and Lovis Estey.)

The Sayles Dairy Farms' Ice Cream and Milk Bar, shown here from Holbrook Avenue about 1950, enclosed the window service area along South Washington Street and added tables and booths. Window service was still available along the northerly side of the building. In the 1960s, Gordon Pepper ran Gordon's Dairy Bar here. The building was torn down and replaced by a gas station, which lasted only a short time. The Sun Chronicle office is currently located on this site. (Photograph courtesy of Ervin and Lovis Estey.)

The Snack Shack straddled the Plainville-North Attleborough town line along Kelley Boulevard at the northwest corner of Plain Street. Here in the 1950s and '60s you could enjoy a simple meal or ice cream while you watched the activity at Wilkins Airport across Route 152. (Photograph courtesy of Gregg Dorrance.)

Morin's Lakeside, seen here after it burned in 1960, was located on Bungy Road near the Mansfield-North Attleborough town line. Here you could enjoy dancing to live music or the views of Bungy Lake from its verandas. When it was Edwards', you could also watch bathers dive or jump off of the tower on the floating diving pier that was located just behind the building.

Seven

Service to Town, State, and Nation

Winifred Capwell (the driver at left) and Hugh McCretton (the assistant foreman at right) gallop away from the Falls Fire Station in Hose 2. In 1913, about when this photograph was taken, four fire companies serviced the town. Chemical and Hose Co. No. 1 and Hook and Ladder Co. No. 1 were located at the Fisher Street Fire Station. Hose Co. No. 2 was located at the Attleboro Falls Fire Station. Hose Co. No. 3 was located on Old Post Road in the Oldtown Fire Station.

This picture of the Attleboro Falls Fire Station was taken in 1975, just two years before it closed. In 1977, the town was serviced by three fire stations. The station on Kelley Boulevard had just recently been opened and the Falls Fire Station was on its way out.

The firemen of the Oldtown Fire Station posed for this photograph on April 5, 1931, not long before the station was abandoned. On the ladder wagon at left we have, from left to right, driver Henry Todd, Frank Hunt, Edward Fuller, and D. Henry Hunt. On the hose wagon at right are, from left to right, driver Samuel McCartney, Lt. Henry Slaiger, and Captain George W. Todd. The Oldtown Fire Station was located on the easterly side of Old Post Road, just north of house number 506.

The old hand-tub Pioneer, long since replaced by steam pumpers and fire hydrants, was relegated to parade duty as seen here in September of 1910. James M. Day drives the team as George Warren oversees. Pioneer is currently housed in the Falls Fire Barn Museum.

Here is Mr. Capwell (see p. 99) at the reins of Hose 1 in front of the Fisher Street Fire Station about 1900. He moved to the Attleboro Falls Fire Station some time about 1913, when he moved his home from a house near Fisher Street on Mt. Hope Street to 172 Commonwealth Avenue. The Fisher Street Fire Station was the fire headquarters until the present station on Elm Street opened in 1930. This station burned in 1894 and again in 1940, after it had been abandoned.

This is the Fisher Street Fire Station about 1920. It was located on the northerly side of Fisher Street, just west of the Ten Mile River. The police had some lockup cells in the basement. The late great Harry Houdini, bound and handcuffed, escaped from a cell here. From left to right in the front of the truck are Thomas Casey, Eugene Henshaw, an unidentified man, Harold Henshaw, and William White. The rest remain unidentified.

The Central Fire Station on Elm Street is decorated for the tercentenary parade in this photograph taken on September 13, 1930. The station had only been open since February of that year. Engine 1, at far left, is a 1925 Maxim, manufactured in Middleboro, MA. Next is the chief's brand new Ford Model A Phaeton. Next are Hose 1 and Ladder 1, moved here from the Fisher Street Station (now closed). The two horse-drawn wagons from the Oldtown Station were here only for the photograph. This station never housed horse-drawn wagons.

This photograph was taken on the occasion of Kenny Bragg being appointed deputy chief. The following have been identified, from left to right: (front row) Kenny Bragg, engineer Fred Sturdy, Bill McDonald, Lt. Joe Turley, and engineer Irving Linley; (back row) Call Captain Bill White, Eugene Sherman, Alex Parks, Marcellus Chandler, Harold Henshaw, Ray Keyes, Jim Cleary, and Henry Meyer. Engineer was the term given to fire commissioners of the time.

Here we have the "men in blue" at a black-tie affair; the annual concert and ball to benefit the Police Relief Association at Red Men's Hall (see p. 125) in 1947. Pictured are the following, from left to right: (seated) James McGowan, Carl McDonald, Chief Peter J. McKeon, Joseph A. McAvoy, and Joseph Lacasse; (standing) George Elliott, Stanley Lykus, John Coyle, Norman Watters, and Arthur Irvine.

Posing in this photograph, taken in front of the Mason Avenue Police Station soon after it was built in 1936, are the following, from left to right: (seated) Louis Rogovers, Russell Greer, William Soyer, Chief Peter McKeon, Jack Brown, Alfred Salt, Frank Frey, and Frank Frobel; (standing, second row) Carl MacDonald, Herman Thiele, Pat Donnelly, Joe McAvoy, Jack McCarthy, Mike Lorden, Wilfred Messier, Henry Liebrich, Tom Casey, and Adelard Ringuette; (third row) Norman Watters, Fred Dietrich, and Henry Irvine; (back) John Smith.

In the 1940s, the police station was remodeled and added to. An addition toward North Washington housed the MacKreth Memorial Emergency Hospital, staffed by nurse Miss Rose Brennan. The doorway at right in this photograph was the entrance to the police station.

The privately owned North Attleborough Water Company was incorporated in 1883 and its first well (pictured here) was completed in 1889 at a cost of $4,789. The well was 30 feet deep and 28 feet in diameter. It supplied water to a tank constructed on "Watery Hill," Elmwood Street. Besides residential customers, it also supplied the private Fire District No. 1. At a special town meeting in 1892, the town purchased the two private concerns.

When the townspeople of North Attleborough felt that they were being overcharged for natural gas and electricity, they voted to establish a town-owned electric company in 1894. Posing in this 1965 photograph are, from left to right, North Attleborough Electric linemen Dick Coffey, Bob Veilleux, Al George, Guido Feccia (kneeling), Mal Hood, and Bob Hiltz, after receiving training from the instructor at far right.

Bentley Ware of Plainville, a stationary engineer for North Attleborough, drives the Buffalo-Pitts steamroller past the Emerson House. In the days before automobiles, a man waving a red flag preceded the steamroller to warn horse-drawn vehicles of its approach. Mr. Ware ran a cider mill in Plainville and the steam engine that brought ice into Ira Richards' icehouse on Whiting's Pond.

The Powder House, located off Mt. Hope Street opposite Linden, was erected in 1768. Built by the Town of Attleborough for munitions storage, it was used during the Revolutionary War and the War of 1812. Except for the addition of a fence, it remains essentially the same as in this 1905 view.

Members of the Prentiss M. Whiting Post of the Grand Army of the Republic pose for a picture in front of the J.D. Pierce School, which was located diagonally across the street from the GAR Hall. Each Memorial Day they turned out to honor the war dead. The custom continued until the last member, Michael Harlow, who served in the Calvary and Navy and may be the gentleman wielding the sword, died in 1939.

One hundred and five members of Company I, 7th Regiment Massachusetts Volunteers, the first from Attleborough to be mustered into service on June 15, 1861, were given a rousing send off from the Baptist Common as they left for training at a camp in Taunton. First Sergeant Prentiss Whiting was among those who left, but did not return. GAR members assembled for this picture at the Baptist church after the Civil War. (Photograph courtesy of Dave Nicholson.)

This group led the parade to the dedication of the Civil War Monument. The police officers are, from left to right, Arthur Reed, Jesse Stevens, and Charles Howard. On horseback are Louis Freeman, John Bliek (parade marshal and superintendent of the Town Poor Farm), Robert J. Fuller (superintendent of schools), and Louis Franklin. John E. Miner's furniture store and Tufts Tool Shop (see p. 55) are in the background.

This crowd awaits the services that would lead to the unveiling of the Civil War Monument on the Baptist Common on November 11, 1911. The order of exercises included the singing of "Our Boys in Blue," an ode written expressly for the occasion, the invocation by Rev. George E. Osgood, the unveiling, the singing of "The Star Spangled Banner" and "America" by schoolchildren, an oration by J. Payson Bradley (past dept. commander of the Mass. GAR), singing by the German Singing Society (see p. 126), and the benediction of Rev. Zenas Crowell.

In June of 1898 the men of Co. I, which included residents of Attleborough and North Attleborough, were mustered into the service of the U.S. during the Spanish-American War. They gathered in front of the Second Congregational Church on Park Street in Attleborough. This was the "White Church," since replaced by a brick structure and the elevating of the railroad tracks.

Posed in front of the GAR Hall during World War I, these Red Cross volunteers were about to canvass the town for money. Shown are, from left to right, as follows: (front row) Katherine Armstrong, Lois Leiper, Grace King, Isabel Manchester, Jennie Maintien, Helen Bishop, Elizabeth Noble, Vivian White, and Eleanor Ball; (middle row) Florence Bell, two unidentified women, Marion Peckham, Helen Whiting, Hazel Scanlon, Bertha Brown, and Bonnie Myers; (back row) Mr. Sunderland, Percy Ball, St. Elmo Coombs, John Tweedy, Mr. Baker, and Gilbert Weller.

On July 4, 1919, the town of North Attleborough sponsored a parade to welcome their heroes home from World War I. Members from every branch of the service passed through the Welcome Home arch constructed across North Washington Street from the vacant lot where the Emerson House had stood to the Boyle Block. At a banquet after the parade, each man and woman who served was given a bronze medal from the grateful citizens of North Attleborough.

John F. Mason Jr. (shown here second from the right in the back row) was another of the airmen from North Attleborough who did not return from World War II (see p. 2). Jackie, the son of John and Marion Mason, was killed on the day after his 21st birthday on a bombing run over Hungary. Staff Sergeant Mason was the engineer and gunner on a B-24. Jack's brother Charlie, wounded in Italy, returned home at the end of the war.

In September of 1939, Joseph W. Martin Jr. (third from left) returned home from Washington D.C., where he was Republican leader of Congress, to present Ed McGowan an award for community service. The following were also present, from left to right: Walter Simms, Ernest Bliek, State Senator Jarvis Hunt (in white), State Representative Frank Kelley, and George Leven.

Jarvis Hunt served in the state senate from 1936 to 1948 (he became president of the state senate in 1940). Jarvis was town council for many years. As a small child, he laid the first block in constructing the brick Evening Chronicle Building on Church Street, where his father, Harry, was publisher. Harry later sold the paper to Joseph W. Martin Jr.

Martin for Congress

Primaries September 9th

To the People of North Attleborough:

The present Congressional campaign is of such vital importance to the people of North Attleborough that I am sending this personal communication.

The Attleboro's have never had a representative in Congress. The Jewelry industry is one which needs constant watchfulness in Washington if it is to be prosperous. The present congressman is unable to give the service which is necessary.

The opportunity is now presented to elect a North Attleboro man. It is distinctly to the advantage of every resident of the jewelry district to bring this about. It is so desirable I have no hesitation in appealing to every man and woman to enlist in this fight. It really is your fight as well as mine. I am but the leader of the cause. When you help me you also help yourself and the community.

This contest will be settled in the Republican primary on September 9. If nominated the election will follow without trouble. If we fail to win the primary the fight ends.

Coming as I do from a town in the extreme end of a big district it is a hard uphill fight. To win it is necessary for every man and woman to go to the primary and vote. It will take but a few minutes and as a patriotic citizen interested in good government and the welfare of your town I urge you to make the effort.

If every citizen here will do his duty victory will be won. The polls open September 9 in Memorial hall from 10 A.M. to 8 P.M.

Sincerely yours,

JOSEPH W. MARTIN, Jr.

Joseph W. Martin Jr. started his political career in a 1911 run for the Massachusetts State Legislature. In 1924, he set his sights on Washington D.C. This letter is from that campaign. Joe went on to serve in the U.S. House of Representatives from 1925 to 1966. He was the Republican leader for many of those years and Speaker of the House under Presidents Harry S. Truman and Dwight D. Eisenhower.

These North Attleborough civic leaders are, from left to right, Dr. Charles A. Bowman (Kiwanis Club president), Gerald E. Riley (the town selectman and chairman for the event), Mrs. Margaret Wood (representing the Merchants' Association), and Harry Sperry of the Rotary Club. The group worked on the arrangements for a testimonial dinner for Joe Martin held at the King Philip Ballroom in Wrentham on June 1, 1953.

Seven
The Town Social

What little boy does not enjoy playing in mud puddles? Here a group of boys play along the Seven Mile River in 1894. The bridge in the background is part of Draper Road, connecting Old Post Road (which would be down the road to the right) to South Washington Street (to the left). This section of Draper Road still remains quite natural with scenic stone walls and plenty of vegetation; however, the Cinema and a busy Route 1 are now just a short distance beyond.

Reservoir Street, the road between the lower (to the left) and upper portions of Falls Pond, seems to have always been there. The pond was created by the damming of the Ten Mile River in Attleborough Falls in 1831. The road shows up on a map of Attleborough in 1832. This picture of two people fishing in the upper pond in 1907 wouldn't look much different if it were taken today.

This is another view of the lower portion of the Falls Pond. The c. 1900 photograph was taken looking north from the dam. The four identical houses at right were mill houses for Daggett's Braid Mill (see p. 59). The hill seen just over the mill houses is known as Peck's Mountain. The houses at the center are along Peck Street.

The Angle Tree Stone has always been a popular place to visit. The stone monument was erected in 1790 at the site of the original Angle Tree, which marked the southernmost boundary of the Massachusetts and Plymouth Colonies. The stone is located up a dirt road off of Upper High Street, just beyond the curve in the road after the intersection of Ellis Road. (Photograph courtesy of John DeGrafft.)

Flowerpot Rock, located on Red Rock Hill until being removed for the construction of Wal-Mart, was once a favorite spot for picnickers. It is another of the landmarks now missing from Route 1.

This "tintype" view of the Celtic Cornet Band of North Attleborough, taken about 1870, shows the band lined up in what was known as Kendall's Grove. Kendall's Grove was located in the area along Church Street, seen in the background, from behind the Odd Fellows Building all the way up to house that is now the rectory of Sacred Heart Church.

Some of the best trotters and pacers in the country competed at the fair grounds in Attleborough Falls during the four days of October that the fair was held here. The grounds were located on the northerly side of Commonwealth Avenue east of Burden Avenue and included a portion of the land that is now Triboro-Plaza. (Photograph courtesy of Attleboro Industrial Museum.)

This picture of the "Butchers Association" was taken from the infield of the track, with the camera looking west toward Commonwealth Avenue. North Avenue joins Commonwealth just behind the large tree at the left in this 1893 photograph. There appears to be a parade of delivery wagons going around the track. There were only seven butchers, meat markets, and provisioners listed in the 1894 directory!

The buildings and fair grounds were dedicated on September 20, 1871, and the first fair was held the following month. The first floor of Agricultural Hall, pictured here about 1880, was used for agricultural exhibits during the fair. The second floor was used for meetings not only during the fair, but also for those of the Farmers and Mechanics Association, later reorganized as the Attleborough Agricultural Association, the rest of the year. The fairs stopped some time before 1910.

The cornerstone of the Richards Memorial Library was laid on June 16, 1894, and the building was completed in 1895. The books were moved from the Boyle Block (see p. 64), where the library had been located since the town took over a privately run lending library in 1889. The Renaissance styling of the building, shown here in 1910, has been maintained in the additions to the rear of the building made in 1929 and 1965.

Anna L. Tweedy, Harriet T. Richards, and E. Ira Richards donated the land, building, and furnishings of the Richards Memorial Library to the town of North Attleborough in memory of their parents, Edmund Ira and Lucy Morse Richards. The portraits of Lucy and Edmund Ira grace the reading room, seen here in 1910. This room remains much the same today, with the exception of the gas lighting and the addition of plush couches.

Edgar Starkey operated a poolroom on the second floor and a bowling alley and cigar store on the first floor of the old Academy Building (see p. 64). Starkey also operated the theater at right until it was purchased by the Elm Amusement Co. of Boston in 1920 and renamed the Elm Theater. The theater not only showed the new moving pictures, but live vaudeville acts as well. The old Academy Building was destroyed by fire in March 1915. The vacant building that once housed the Sentry Bank and Rite Aid Drug Store is here now.

The Community Theater opened in 1929 and almost immediately ran into the financial troubles of the 1930s. During the 1950s, shows changed three times a week and also included minstrel shows. The theater was the site of many a lively town meeting. A metal police officer, a gift of the Coca-Cola Company, guarded the crosswalk in this 1968 photograph. (Photograph courtesy of Alan Bliek.)

The Boro Drive In Theater opened about 1948 during the boom of this type of enterprise. This theater attracted away much of the business from the smaller, indoor theaters like that of the Community Theater. A small playground was also provided to entertain the youngsters while you waited for it to get dark enough for the show to start. The Boro went the way of most drive-ins when the multi-plex theaters sprang up in the 1970s. It was finally removed to make way for the Bradlees Plaza.

Jolly Cholly Funland, located on East Washington Street across from the present location of Stop & Shop, was THE summertime destination in the 1960s. It not only provided entertainment for the youngsters of the area, but was also likely to provide them with their first job. Charles Nasif started by selling ice cream here. Over the years, he added pizza, hamburgers, and the kiddie rides. During the 1970s, a flea market was held in the rear parking lots here.

Bud Tongue (seen here at right with his wife, Barbara) operated a television store in the Hancock Building (see p. 64) in the 1950s. Radio and TV personalities Hum and Strum (at center) attended the grand opening of the store. A crowd of people filled the sidewalk to watch Hum and Strum perform.

In the 1950s and '60s, Al Trembley ran Friday night auctions in his North End Auction Barn at the old Everett Estate. Joseph Barden owned the house on Park Street, near the corner of Everett Street, when this photograph was taken about 1905.

Planes started landing at the Wilkins' family farm some time in the 1930s. In this September 1940 photograph, planes have landed at the rear of their Seven Elms Dairy Farm, which was located on Messenger Street in Plainville. The airport closed during the war years and re-opened under the management of Russ Carlton and Lloyd Whitney after the war.

The Wilkins' Airport never took off the way the operators had expected. By the 1970s, when this photograph was taken, the airport was only a memory. Most of the land west of Route 152 in this photograph, much of it in North Attleborough, was once part of the airport property.

Paul Revere chartered the Bristol Lodge in 1797. The Lodge, originally located in the town of Norton, moved to North Attleborough in 1830. This Masonic Hall building, built in 1876 and pictured about 1910, burned along with the Academy Building (see p. 120) on March 12, 1915. Meetings were held in the Odd Fellows Building until their present building was completed in 1928.

The Aurora Lodge of the Independent Order of Odd Fellows was instituted in 1846. The Odd Fellows Building, pictured here soon after it was erected in 1874–5, is located on the corner of North Washington and Church Streets. In the 1890s, the present facade and tower were added along North Washington Street.

The Mirimichi Tribe No. 110, Improved Order of Red Men, was instituted in 1893. Their meeting place, Red Men's Hall, seen here about 1910, was located on the northerly side of Church Street, just west of the Universalist church. Dancing schools and wrestling matches were among the activities held here.

The Red Men used to have a torch parade during which they would dress up in their regalia and dance down the main street. Here they are seen lined up at the foot of Hunting Street. Among those pictured are Fred Bartlett, Fred Caswell, Burt Palmer, Charles McLoughlan, Elmer Blake, William McKell, Frank Frobel, William Parks, Peter Frasier, Gene Freeman, Max Rosenberg, Charles Pilling, Joe Evans, Harry Hartman, Benjamin Armstrong, and Arthur Blackinton.

Within a year after this Benevolent Protective Order of Elks float appeared in the 1913 July Fourth Parade, the Elks laid the cornerstone of their building on Church Street, just north of the Red Men's Hall. After the Red Men disbanded, the Elks purchased their building in 1940 and connected the two buildings together. Both buildings are now gone, having been replaced by an apartment building and parking lot.

The Frohsinn Singing Society, incorporated in 1888, owned this building on Smith Street, pictured in 1908. The second floor had a balcony that went all the way around the building and opened in the center to the first floor. Each Christmas season they would decorate a tree that rose from the first floor and went past the second-floor balcony. The group seems to have disbanded when the U.S. entered the World War in 1917. The building is now an apartment house and is located just south of the Town Garage.

Constructed mainly with volunteer help, Camp Shady Pines Girl Scout Camp opened to campers on August 4, 1941. It operated for over 25 years under the watchful direction of Ruth Rhind. Swimming in Abbott Run was among the activities at the camp. Aqua ballet was the highlight of Parents' Night. (Photograph courtesy of Nancy Rhind Parks.)

These young men of the North Attleborough YMCA perform in the old GAR Memorial Hall, located on the southerly side of Elm Street, near the intersection of Route 1. The YMCA occupied this building until the building on Elmwood Street was completed in the 1974. In 1975, the old building was torn down.

The 1913 July Fourth Parade seems to have been one of the largest ever held in North Attleborough. This is the float sponsored by the Webster Co. The boy in front, with bottle in hand, prepares to christen the ship, appropriately named Sterling.

The Columbia Bicycle Club financed this 1890s semi-professional team, which gave Columbia Field its name. Babe Ruth, Walter Johnson, and Jim Thorpe were among the professionals that played here during "Little World Series" games organized and financed by industrialists from the rival towns of Attleboro and North Attleborough.

Gus Flynn's stars of the North Attleborough WPA League of the late 1930s, shown here at Columbia Field, included the following, from left to right: (front row) Archie Walden, Phil and Bud Suprenant, John Slowey, Ralph Hall, Randy Moore, Midge Hall, and Tony DiFiore; (middle row) Joe Kelley, Stan Skolski, Walt Bronowski, Leon Peao, Al Schickle, Bucky Jones, Eddie Rioux, and Gus Flynn; (back row) Ray Slowey, Dick Phippen, Ted White, Art Gaskin, Phil Fontaine, Bud Greene, Eddie Sekowski, and Chick Germaine.

Brothers Jim and Bob Munroe are among those in this 1930s picture of the Townies semi-professional football team. Bob is in the middle of the third row; Jim, who was a member of the Brown football team that played in the first Rose Bowl Game, is at the extreme right in the first row.